Echoes of Existence

Ritika Das

BookLeaf Publishing

India | USA | UK

Presentation by *BookLeaf Publishing*

Web: www.bookleafpub.com

E-mail: info@bookleafpub.com

ISBN: 9789360946081

First edition 2024

CONTENTS

Acknowledgement

About the Author

PREFACE

Welcome to the captivating journey that lies within the pages of "Echoes of Existence." As you lose yourself in these verses, I invite you to delve into my world, where the seemingly ordinary undergoes a remarkable transformation into something extraordinary. In these poems, I offer you a glimpse into my appreciation for the mundane, where even the smallest of things are noticed, cherished, and celebrated.

As a lifelong lover of words, I have embarked on a mission to cultivate a culture of joy and introspection through my first poetry collection. I believe that every experience, no matter how small, carries the potential for profound meaning. Through these lines, I hope to remind you that each day, we are all participants in a collective journey where our shared emotions bind us together.

My ultimate wish is for you to uncover inspiration and develop a heightened appreciation for the world that surrounds you. Within these poems, you will discover the power of simplicity and the resonance it holds in our lives. I am honoured that you have chosen to accompany me on this relatable and soul-stirring expedition, and I sincerely hope that you find resonance within the echoes of life's moments.

With heartfelt gratitude,
Ritika Das

From Dreams to Reality: Navigating Adulthood

Adulting, this wretched land where all our
dreams got misplaced,
Where once we chased the impulse of childhood
with a smile on our face.

Now stuck in an eternal maze that we never
meant to solve,
Our dreams replaced by mountains of laundry,
which do not self-dissolve.

How we dreamt of skipping stages, assuming we
will stay young and free,
But the monstrous bills came knocking loudly,
hit us with a harsh reality.
Back then, our scraped knees healed with
laughter, a band-aid and a hug,
Now we are troubled with anxiety and mental
health seems to be a never-ending bug.

Art projects and comics have turned into Sunday
afternoon naps,
We have successfully traded our hobbies for
adulting, what an awful trap!
Those hours of window-shopping, for things
fancy and bright,
Now switched to dull grocery lists, it is a
different kind of sight.

Each month the bills come back to haunt us, a
never-ending horror movie script,
Snatching all our hard-earned savings, leaving
our pockets bare and stripped.
The paycheck comes and disappears, what a
fleeting, disloyal friend,

Who seduced us into a web of life-style
spending, which now never seems to end.

But hey, at least there are others; we are not
alone in this horrid scene,
Maybe someone will someday invent an app, to
help us with a grown-up routine.
With daily sustenance as our only compass, we
attempt to challenge the craze,
This adulting adventure has gone too far, but we
have come to accept the glaze.

And hence, we raise a glass to all the grown-up
chaos and fun,
We embrace the unexpected twists and turns,
until life is truly done.
For in this world of grown-ups, where dreams
and laughter ultimately meet,
We will find our own happy ending, even though
the path may be a little bitter-sweet.

Battle of the Morning Alarm

Each morning, the devil's whisper summons me
from my slumber,
The alarm clock, that blinking beast, ringing a
beep with hazy numbers.
It screams at dawn, a cruel imposter visiting in
the morning light,
Wrenching me from dreams with all its panic
and fright.

I try to snooze, I try to escape its persistent and
terrifying call,
But after the first two warnings, it gets shriller
and starts to bawl.
A reality check wrapped, in its glaring numbers
and piercing tones,
They remind me of my responsibilities, of
labour and corporate chores.

The grumpy mask I wear each morning is a gift
of the shrill voice,
For who can wake with joy when jerked from
sleep, not given a choice?
Choosing between tones that soothe but fail to
wake,
Or ones that blare like sirens, capable of causing
a quake.

Mondays especially sting, with that dreadful
morning call,
It's an orchestra of chaos and turmoil, and a
stressful, deafening brawl.
But amid all the grumbling, I fail to see its
worth,
The unsung hero of my morning, my alarm
clock driving me forth.

The red numbers glow harder, burning into my
sleepy gaze,

They are an assault on my bodily senses, a
tormenting way to raise.
My body resists, my back aches as I fumble
from my bed,
The alarm clock's oppressing song still echoing
in my head.

A few more minutes later, I find the courage to
leave my blanket behind,
To face the harsh corporate world, to wake my
wavering mind.
And as the evil grin softens, I assume my alarm
smiles through its eyes,
I come to realize, it was my friend all along, in
the devil's disguise.

Beyond The Silence

In the world of communication, where words
often fail,
Exists a language more profound, that hides and
leaves no trail.
Silence, the anonymous ally who often goes
unseen,
Speaks volumes when loud voices leave a space
in between.

Gestures take the main stage when words take a
backseat,
An eye-roll speaks louder; nods affirm the
secrets we keep.

Silence rules in the reading rooms, the language
officially-approved,
Hushes are whispered, voices muffled, and
noises are removed.

Sharpened senses listen, the world has a clearer
view,
For silence lets us truly hear what words can't
always do.
And peace finds a quiet corner, where chatter
fades away,
The language of stillness whispers prudence to
us all day.

Introverts find comfort in quiet's gentle hold,
A space for their thoughts to unfold, for stories
yet untold.
Snowflakes falling softly, whispers on the
breeze,
Silence paints a picture where worries find
release.

And when mountains are whispering to the
wind, and stars are twinkling in the silence,
Hush-hush will hold its breath, waiting for the
next sound to come to our defense.
For in silence, we find peace, and our words
drift away,

It is the language of stillness, where calmness
always finds a way.

A Cup of Comfort

The brain fog clinging to my head, a struggle to
see clear,
A steaming mug appears, banishing all my fear.
The first sip, a swirl of creaminess, like a warm
hug in a cup,
Nudging me out of slumber, enticing me to wake
up.

Coffee, my personal motivator that speaks with
every sip,
"Bean there, done that" it says, a vanilla-like
trip.
Before coffee enters my tummy, conversations
are but mumbles,
My words turn into rambling, and my thoughts
turn into a jumble.

But as caffeine rushes through my veins, I see
myself transform,
From an arrogant figure into a human, nice and
warm.
It's more than just a drink, you see, a bittersweet
delight,
A personalized caramel cloud, to chase away the
night.

The first smell of the brew reminds me of life's
possibilities,
The potential that lies ahead, that courage to
fight hostilities.
Coffee encourages me to express myself,
unfiltered and free,
Before society convinces me to blend in, filter
and agree.

The clinking spoon, the hissing milk, the mug
warm in my hand,
A symphony of morning sounds, in this
delightful land.
Each sip a moment to embrace, a gentle,
warming friend,
Coffee whispers, "You've got this, adulting's just
pretend."

Morning miracles in a cup and instant
gratification every day,

A lifeline that directs me into a functioning
human fray,
This creamy hug in a porcelain mug is a
confidence boost so strong,
Coffee is the liquid remedy that makes adulting
a joyful song.

Roadmaps of Change

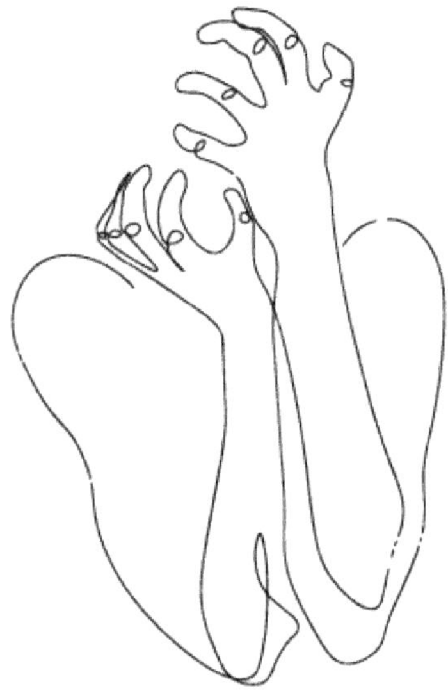

The future is a canvas where every day a new
mystery is cast,
There are plot twists and turns, and the narrative
is shockingly vast.
Each passing year is a new level to conquer, a
higher standard to reach,
The difficulty level escalates, my eyes cry but
the panic escapes my speech.

Once, I thought Career "A" would be my
"happily-ever-after" song,

Now laughter echoes, that path's a joke, where I
don't truly belong.
I find myself constantly reinventing, comfort
zone's a thing of the past,
Trembling with fear and taking huge leaps, my
opportunities turn up at last.

Each job assignment is supposed to be a learning
curve new,
I unlearn and relearn the drill, to reach the goal I
aim to pursue.
Embracing the "ouch" moments in my life, all
the stumbles along the way,
While my people cheer and comfort, reminding
me to go on, come what may.

The inner voice of doubt crouches silently, like a
whisper in the night,
When coffee shoots up the anxiety, and
late-night study turns into a fight.
There are butterflies in my stomach, as I watch
future possibilities unfold,
My career stretching boundaries, my dreams
waiting for me to be bold.

And so, like a chameleon, I blend into my
dreams and change my hues,
And braver steps are taken, as I beat my Monday
blues.

The road ahead is full of twists, I am totally
aware,
Yet I embrace the unknown, and for further
challenges I prepare.

From Anxiety to Achievement: Journey of My To-do List

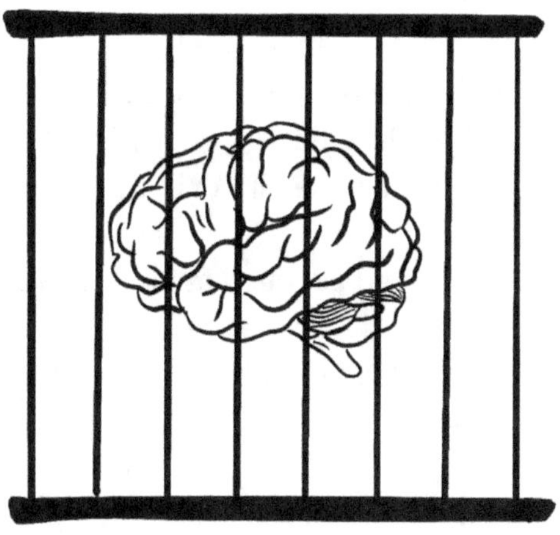

In the tiny world of procrastination, my to-do list silently lurks,
It mirrors my threat and anxiety, there seem to be no visible perks.
So I push it aside, and hope it will vanish, like smoke in this crowded air,
But deadlines hover with an angry sprint, and there's chaos everywhere.

As a perfectionist, my to-do list turns into a
measure,
Of my productivity and competence, it's quite a
quest for treasure.
Each task must be flawless and accurately
planned,
But perfection's hold on me tightens, creating an
endless demand.

Then a realist's perspective emerges, and
acknowledges the cost,
My to-do list is a necessary evil, it's a war I've
won but lost.
One by one, I start conquering my list, with
focus and with might,
Trying to keep the turmoil at bay, until the finish
line is in sight.

The optimist in me whispers quietly, halfway
through the battle,
Reminds me the list is a roadmap, it will guide
me through all of life's tattle.
And helps me focus on growth and achievement,
my checkmarks glowing bright,
Each crossed-off task on my to-do list, brings
me closer to dreams in sight.

These roles I play, shifting within myself, while
I also strive and learn,

That my to-do list is my best friend, my
accomplice through twists and turns.
Think of crisp paper, and pastel highlighters, and
sticky notes on display,
This army of organizing essentials, leading me
all the way.

But sometimes, the list stares back at me, with
judgment in its gaze,
For there are loads of unfinished tasks, and I get
stuck in an ambitious maze.
I warn myself that it's okay to let go, I need not
conquer every line,
The list can rest, just like I need to, and it's
going to be just fine.

So I embrace its flaws and accept my
imperfections, as much possible with grace,
With newfound appreciation, I dance through the
chaos, finding my solace.
For my to-do list might appear to be mundane,
humble, and small,
But holds the power to keep me going, and helps
me never stall.

The Power of Pause

In the heart of office chaos, where clouds of deadlines loom,
And the incessant calls and emails, simply add up to my gloom,
There exists a tiny corner, overlooked, quaint and small,
A cozy nook tucked away, where my peace finds its call.

By the window, overlooking the city's simmering sight,

Buildings touching high, and gardens
shimmering bright.
Here, eagles gracefully soar, making nests of
their own,
While the corporate world buzzes, this corner
stands alone.

In the intervals of my work chores, here my
sanctuary lies,
A place where I escape, finding solace in
disguise.
Stealing moments for a coffee break, a corner of
temporary resort,
Witnessing a world that slows down, as my tired
soul retorts.

Within this hidden shelter, I relish every single
sip,
The aroma performs a waltz, and the caffeine
makes me flip.
Seated at an empty desk, with a closed laptop in
sight,
As the sunlight streams through the window,
casting a golden light.

While the distant hum of traffic fades into the
breeze,
I take deep breaths, and manage to find some
inner calm and ease.

In that small, serene corner, I lose myself for a
while,
Relaxing in the glory of a caffeine-induced
smile.

Who knew a simple cup of joy, paired with a
tranquil view,
Could bring me temporary sanity, helping me
see through.
The hurricane of deadlines and emails, a
deranged and chaotic tide,
With each sip, finding peace, on this unexpected
ride.

So, find your own sweet haven, among this
medley we call work-life,
Seek out your own little corner, escape the hustle
and the strife.
With the world outside your window, and the
depths of your soul within,
You might discover true peace, to help you
reignite and begin.

The Lunchtime Dilemma

Allow me to share the story of a busy, forgetful
day,
When lunch slipped my mind, and my tummy
turned stray.
As the morning raced on, my growling stomach
awoke,
There was a troop of hunger to handle, a cry that
I couldn't revoke.

A dull throb in my head, a sign of diminishing
power,

Low blood sugar's revenge, growing stronger by
the hour.
The quick clicks of the keyboard, now slowed
down to a crawl,
The rhythm of my typing faltered; my energy
began to fall.

Then distracted snacking happened, unhealthy
choices in my hand,
Chips, candy and cola; but to my tummy, all
three were bland.
From the desks of my colleagues, tempting
aroma drifted near,
Spices, bread, and coffee; the mockery was
crueller than I feared.

The computer screen blurred at the edges, this
was getting out of league,
Signs of hunger consumed me, leaving me
mentally stale and fatigued.
Productivity plummeted and crashed, like drops
against a stone,
The consequence of skipping lunch is now a
lesson to me well-known.

As I devour my lunch, I want this to continue
being a reminder,
Of honouring how special is the lunch break, to
let ourselves be kinder.

To nourish the body and mind, so that they
string together and thrive,
For lunchtime is also an escape, a chance to
pause and to feel alive.

With Rain as Reminder

Sitting in a cozy café, on a gloomy, rainy day,
I hide in refuge, eager to chase the clouds away.
Sipping my hot chocolate, the steam dancing in
the air,
As raindrops tiptoe against the window, such a
gentle affair.

The aroma of freshly-brewed coffee, engulfs my
heightened senses,
The soft murmur of conversations, breaking
through emotional fences.

Embracing the present, I find comfort in this
scene,
And a reminder that true significance lies in
ordinary routine.

Instagram-worthy or not, it does not matter to
me,
For it's what we capture through our hearts, that
allows us to see.
The vibrant colours, the smiling faces, laughter
and its sweet sound,
Simple pleasures of life that make my world go
around.

Crashing waves in the distance, and the gentle
sounds of breath,
The melody of soft music, soothing the soul into
various depths.
The smell of croissants, freshly baked, with
kindness and with love,
The blissful earthy scent and heavenly fragrance
from above.

I think about walking on soft grass, feeling the
earth beneath my feet,
And oh, warm sand between my toes, moments
that ground me and complete.
The feeling of belonging, the warm embrace of a
loved one's hug,

A reassuring emotion, the boundless feeling of
being unplugged.

And so, I sat there thinking, of the many sombre
reasons,
Of struggling and being absent, through all the
countless seasons.
Where monsoons make some gloomy, they also
make some laugh,
But they surely remind us all, that none else can
live life on your behalf.

Ink-Stained Conversations

Last night, I stumbled upon an old, worn-out
friend,
My diary—full of secrets, from the beginning to
the end.
It took me back to the day when our wholesome
eyes first met,
In a dusty bookstore, I picked her up, a moment
I won't forget.

Wondering whether to take it home, confusion
rang into my ears,
Little did I know that it would hold all my hopes
and fears.
Now battered and overused, with yellowed
pages and faded ink,

It carries the weight of my memories, the tenets
I used to think.

Ink stains and doodles dance on its crumbling
face,
Coffee rings, like galaxies, marking moments in
each space.
Each mark telling a story, a spark of inspiration
or a blunder,
A burst of creativity, a thought stumble that
made me wonder.

Pencil sketches and poems, decorate its fragile
state,
Half-framed sentences, crossed-out lines fill its
brittle fate.
Sticky notes and flags, reminders of temporary
thoughts,
A battle of a thousand words, this diary has so
far fought.

I think my diary smiled back, knowing I hadn't
forgotten,
It whispered in my ear, of dreams that now feel
rotten.
With a gentle nudge, it encouraged me to once
again begin,
To pick up where I left, to embrace my wonders
within.

Resilient Reminders: Navigating Life with Sticky Notes

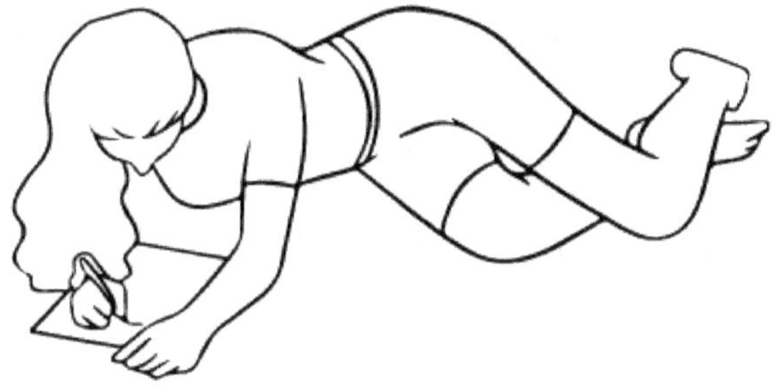

Join along for a day in my life, navigating
through a sea of reminders,
Each sticky note representing parts of me; when
lost, they help me find her.
Each note holds a story, a forgotten appointment,
an inspiring quote,
A doodle created in anxiety, but also a reminder
to stay afloat.

From work deadlines to grocery lists and lengthy personal goals,
These tiny squares are the guide to maintaining order in all my roles.
Passing life with flying colours, but memory is where I fail,
Plagued by ultimate forgetfulness, but with post-it notes, I prevail.

Lifesavers in sticky squares, these colourful little bits,
Like a backup drive for my brain, with memory that never quits.
Some days I'm astonished at how your resistance never shakes,
Even when my shitty memory takes unscheduled coffee breaks.

The pen scratches on the paper, audibly leaving their bold mark,
As I peel off a note, feeling the stickiness, a sensation so stark.
The quiet and happy hums escape me, as I mindlessly jot things down,
Knowing I won't forget, with these little squares around.

So cheers to my sticky notes, my tiny reminders
in glue,
For being the backbone of my days, helping life
ease through.
With you by my helpless side, I navigate
through each day,
With all your colourful reminders, that stick and
never sway.

Whispers of Courage

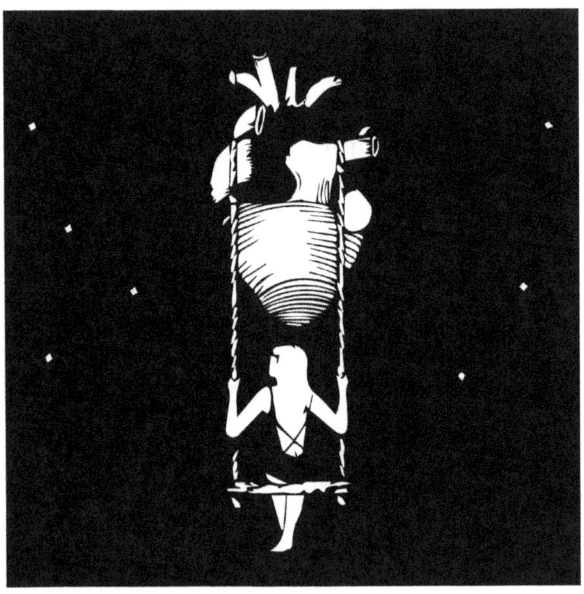

In the territory of life's trials, let me take you on
a journey,
Through the narrative of a young girl whose
dreams suddenly turned awry.
With plans to travel the world, of penning tales
of culture and delight,
Something abruptly shattered her path, she lost
all control of further sight.

Lost her strongest pillar of support, who
understood her wildest dreams,
Now she stood puzzled and angry, uncertain of
where to scream.
People around her, with their good intentions
and well-meaning hearts,
Pushed her towards a path well-known, but a
path far from her true arts.

Lost in the depths of despair, she wandered
aimlessly through her days,
No matter how much she introspected, she
couldn't find her way.
With loved ones by her side, encouraging her to
seek her truth,
She discovered gradual closure, amidst the
turmoil in her youth.

And so, learn to embrace the chaos, when life
throws lemons your way,
You can try to be as fearless, but don't be afraid
to say,
"Help me, for this may be my story, but I can't
face it all on my own."
Lean on your squad, friends, family; you're
never really alone.

And slowly, you'll learn to find laughter, even in
the darkest of nights,

Knowing that tomorrow you'll go back to
reaching bigger heights.
With crumpled tissues and comfort food, let the
tears flow and halt,
For they will slowly heal, and you'll realize it's
not your fault.

Doubts will hold you back, but you'll push past
them with a fight,
For time will stitch your wounds, and will make
everything all right.
There will be times of failure, but there will also
be times of grace,
When you'll find the strength to heal and grow,
you'll find everything you chase.

Beyond Your Inner Critic

There's that feeling of "faking it" as you
navigate your way,
Through the difficult ups and downs of each,
chaotic workday.
Plagued by that inner critic, that loud, relentless
voice,
You end up doubting your worth, it robs you of
your choice.

But here's the thing I've realized, your imposter
isn't a foe,

Maybe just a sidekick, who might just help you
grow.
She adds that sprinkle of spice, and a dash of
drama to your life,
But she's also the reason you stepped up to
embrace your unique drive.

Rejoice in all your achievements, no matter how
tiny or small,
They are a cabinet of your capabilities, a
reminder to always recall.
For we forget to cherish our wins, we assume
they are irrelevant,
But they showcase how we've progressed, our
ambitions and efforts evident.

Comparison is but a trap, to steal your joy and
confidence,
Don't measure your journey against others,
believe in your own competence.
You will find value in your path, your own
rhythm and flow,
For your journey is just as sublime, you need not
be afraid to show.

And as you face your fears and embrace your
inner fragility,
Your authenticity will shine through, you will
power through with humility.

For it is through moments of uncertainty, when
your true self is revealed,
Assurance is part of the journey, you'll find it
and you'll heal.

Let your light sparkle and glow, this feeling is
not your captor,
For in your journey, imposter syndrome is
another passing chapter.
Embrace yourself in totality, with all your talents
and flaws,
And know that you are always enough, just the
way you are.

Weathering the Storm

In the middle of a torrential downpour, a blend
of emotions unfold,
Of a couple engaged in dispute, a war turning
bitter and cold.
Blinded by pride, unable to see each other's truth
with clarity,
Assumptions and insecurities, fuelling the fire to
severity.

Raindrops tapping on the windows, while they
turn away and sulk,

But in solitude comes a moment of reflection,
when memories begin to sculpt.
Each recalls the joy of seasons foregone, when
love was fresh and pure,
They summon their former memories, from a
time when their love was secure.

They regret the verbal bolts they shoved, as they
sat again side-by-side,
Some laughter between their battle, they found
truce in their verbal divide.
With every drop, the anger dissolved; soon
replaced by moist eyes,
With the return of joy, they remembered; if there
are lows, there are also highs.

The rain subsided, smiles were exchanged, and
hearts were thoughtfully mended,
Love endured the storm, and the spite was
calmly ended.
In the whisper of the rain, they found again
peace and resolve,
Over a cup of chai, their affection bubbled and
evolved.

The Struggle for Balance

In the hustle and bustle of life, all the busyness
and the squirm,
Where an exhausted parent tries hard, to keep
their balance firm.
From milk bottles to spreadsheets, their day is
absolutely pinned,
Juggling deadlines and tantrums, their patience
has turned thin.

She's a dedicated office employee, a champion
in many ways,
She burns off all her energy, but "No" she never
says.
On Fridays, when the clock strikes midnight, she
tries not to care,
Promises to fulfil her passions tomorrow, to
reignite a lost flare.

Among the various roles she plays, they all seek
some balance,
A parent, a professional, a woman—isn't she
full of talents?
She squeezes exercise into virtual meetings, and
bribes the kids with phone time,
Finding time to enjoy some laughter, but silently
at unrest in her prime.

She cheers those who manage to transition from
meetings to bedtime stories,
People who seemingly make attempts to actively
tackle all their worries,
Who have no need for an empty inbox, but have
a family dinner time set,
Who symbolize connection and love at home, an
emotion we must not forget.

The ones whose calendars are filled with leisure
and time to have some fun,
Who anticipate their weekends, for solo time
under the sun.
Who share their smiles with loved ones, and
keep notifications turned off,
With soothing music, comfy pee-jays, and hugs
from someone soft.

The woman has learnt that she needs to strive,
for balance in this hectic race,
She must embrace the quirks and strengths that
fill up her life's space.
And if she wants to be among the ones whom
she heartily cheers,
She must learn to say "No" someday, and gulp
down all her fears.

Family Beyond Blood

Today, I'm going to tell you about my
extraordinary clan,
A family of friends, each remarkable, stitched
together over a span.
No siblings of my own, yet they share in my
joys and sorrows,
From life's important milestones to
laughter-filled tomorrows.

They are my chosen relationships, as vital as my
blood ties,

They welcome me with open arms, make me
laugh until I cry.
Our bond, once fastened by joy, further
strengthened by support,
A sense of belonging and acceptance, nothing
short of art.

A medley of backgrounds, cultures, and
experiences unite,
Multiple rays coming together, each one shining
bright.
They know my embarrassing tales, each chapter
and every verse,
With destructive smirks and grins, my
embarrassing stories they rehearse.

Through blunders and through morning breath,
they're still there by my side,
They choose to stay through every fight, their
love they never hide.
Like unpaid therapists, my rants and frustrations
they patiently try to hear,
Their advice, always questionable, but also
always sincere.

With a touch of humour, they turn my everyday
mundane into gold,
Unforgettable moments with them, in memories
I unfold.

They've loved me in spite of all my quirks and
all the idiotic whims,
Accepting me with all my flaws, their love never
seems to slim.

Warm smiles and crinkled eyes, these are our
multiple signs,
That our friendship has blossomed through ages,
creating the sweetest lines.
With all our inside jokes, whispered in gestures,
and all the lunacy we share,
Those movie nights on the couch, and unfiltered
laughter filling the air.

So, here's to raising a toast to the ones who truly
make me whole,
Through the ups and downs of life, they've been
the most beautiful souls.
And even distance can't break, these bonds that
we have formed
With every single reunion, the journey turns
wilder, and also warm.

An Army of Introverts

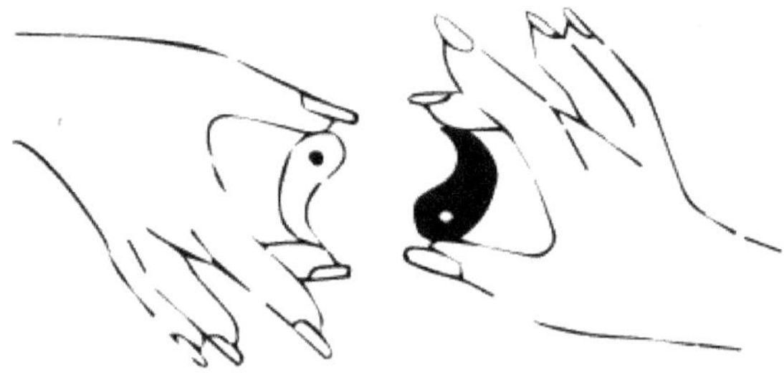

With simplicity and candour, I will try my best
to convey
The beauty of introversion, in every single way.
For as the sun rises in the orange, morning sky,
Introverts awake with a content and peaceful
sigh.

Savouring their coffee, lost in a random thought,
The day's possibilities, slowly filling in all their
slots.

Unlike extroverts who manage to thrive in
crowds,
Solitude is where all the introverts are found.

In the quiet of their own, heavily engaged
minds,
Introverts manage to find their own kind.
They leap at chances to recharge and to
mindfully reflect,
Towards their inner monologue, they try to
self-connect.

Their creative inspiration flourishes in the quiet,
The silence of their surroundings, soothes their
inner riot.
Always lost in some pursuit, their time often
flies by,
Wanting to fulfil their dreams, always aiming for
the sky.

As the moon rises to signal the end of each day,
Introverts retreat to their personal space, from
the crowd away.
They snuggle under fleece blankets, jump into a
comfy bed,
They let their reflections run wild, stuffing up all
their head.

If you were a bit puzzled, I hope that now you
know,
How the inner world looks like, within an
introvert's flow.
And if you, dear reader, are an extrovert—your
words, you must assess,
For I will not be "talking more," maybe you
should talk a little less.

Beautifully Flawed

Imagine a world where perfection takes the spotlight,
Spurring an existence that is standardized and everything is just right.
Wouldn't life go drifting, into dullness and routine?
Living a colourless life, always wondering what could have been.

The cracked ceramic cups, stand in their solitary design,

And still hold our beloved drinks, and they
manage to do just fine.
Those sunrises, streaked with clouds, a scene
candidly pure,
Reminding us that perfection isn't always the
cure.

Militants with scars, chiselled with experiences
past,
Telling us stories of resilience that on their
bodies last.
And what about laughter, uncontrolled and free,
A sound of pure enjoyment, but not "perfection,"
you see.

These imperfections, one day, they whispered in
my ear,
And reminded me of my humanity, the emotion I
hold most dear.
For the world may judge you constantly, with
that critical, tearing gaze,
But I've learned to silence all its deafening craze.

And why even be ashamed of all your tiny
flaws,
They are sprinkles on a cupcake, an unexpected
applause.
Celebrate the beautifully imperfect mess, that is
you,

For your real selves are where all your happiness
brews.
52

The Friday Feels

These bustling streets, on Friday evenings, every
face so upbeat,
This is the day of freedom, the weekends will
soon meet.
And picture all the weary workers, no longer
willing to stay,
As they rush towards their homes, not a moment
to waste away.

In the heart of this city, people have waited long,

Now crowding in cafes and bars, back to places
they belong.
The monotony of the workweek, is now slowly
fading away,
As hysteria fills the bubbling air, every week on
this day.

From behind our work desks, we start to
mentally escape,
Into daydreams and fantasies, our souls begin to
reshape.
The rustling of packing papers, the zipping of
bags in sync,
The preparation to go back home, our spirits all
start to lift.

Counting down the hours and minutes until we
cheer,
The Friday afternoon buzz, still ringing in our
ears.
Happy music on the headphones today, we all
start to groove,
Our weekend clothes await us, the comfort of
which we approve.

We time the clock since midday, everything will
soon be right,
Our mental break will arrive, a respite from the
daily fight.

The weekend, our chance to recharge and to
wilfully restore,
To celebrate all our accomplishments and let all
our hopes pour.

In the anticipation of Friday, as the weekend
closes the race,
We find content and joy, and we rush home to
embrace.
For in this hope-filled anticipation, we are sure
to find,
Possibilities and joys of the weekend,
rejuvenation of our mind.

City Life in Motion

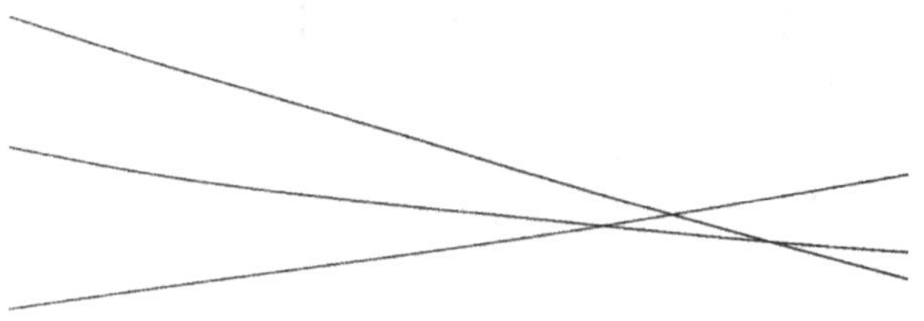

Like every ordinary day, today I take the journey home,
But I see unexpected charm in this city-coloured chrome.
Amidst traffic jams that usually seem to have their own life,

I navigate this experience, and suddenly feel
alive.

From dodging pigeons on sidewalks to crowded,
hustling trains,
Every moment turned into a story, where
boredom could not reign.
Conversations with strangers, and bonds formed
on the go,
Making young connections, and seeds of
friendships sown.

Letting go of control, and flowing with this city's
tide,
Observing every detail, of this city where I
reside.
Amid the urban chaos, I manage to find
gratitude,
For the little joys that end up making my heart
feel renewed.

A seat on the shared cab, traversing paths of
which I'm aware,
The last sip of my coffee, and newfound
prominence in the air.
The destination always mattered, today the
journey etched in my soul,
A rollercoaster of highs and lows, a commute
making me whole.

Sunsets painting streaks of orange and pink over
mighty walls,
Street art whispering stories, the view making
you stall.
Laughter of the children weaving joy into the
urban flow,
And the rustling of newspapers, getting bundled
row by row.

The aroma of street food tempting with flavours
profound,
Spices of curry mixing into the air, those buns
perfectly round.
The metro station holds the history of lives
witnessed over time,
While the traffic lights blink, this city feels like a
rhyme.

And as I arrive home, after all the laughter,
honking, and snacks,
I feel a sense of belonging, as if time had lost its
track.
Applauding the daily commute, which is chaotic
yet strangely lush,
For in these moments, I discovered the allure of
my city, in all its rush.

ACKNOWLEDGEMENT

I am filled with immense gratitude towards all my people who have supported and inspired me throughout the creation of "Echoes of Existence." This poetry collection would not have come to fruition without their unwavering belief in my writing and their invaluable contributions.

First and foremost, my deepest appreciation goes to my family and partner. Your unwavering support and belief in my creative abilities have been the driving force behind these poems. Your encouragement fueled my creative spark and gave me the confidence to share my words with the world.

To my dearest friends, who served as my initial audience, I extend my heartfelt thanks. Your honest feedback and constructive criticism have shaped these poems in countless ways. Your unwavering presence and encouragement have played a significant role in the development of this collection.

A special shoutout goes to my dad. Thank you for always believing in me and teaching me the importance of embracing life's experiences. Your constant wisdom and guidance have been invaluable in my journey as a writer. You have shown me that life is meant to be seized and enjoyed, and your words continue to inspire me everyday.

To my beloved aunt, Kusum Das, I express my deepest gratitude. You have been a constant source of inspiration in the world of writing. Your guidance and encouragement have pushed me to pursue my creativity with every ounce of my being. This book is a testament to the poetry sessions we had during my childhood. I hope that it fills you with pride to see that our shared passion for writing has transformed into a tangible outlet of expression.

Lastly, I want to express my heartfelt gratitude to you, dear reader. Your presence on this journey means the world to me. My utmost hope is that these poems resonate with you, evoke moments of reflection, and bring a smile to your face. Your support and engagement make all the difference.

Thank you all for being part of this incredible journey.

Love and Gratitude.

ABOUT THE AUTHOR

Ritika Das talks about personal growth, well-being and work-life balance and has spent considerable time researching on these topics. Her writing has majorly been showcased through her blog where she writes under her alias "Readably Yours."

She is also a book enthusiast, and you will always find her with a beloved book tucked under her arm. Professionally, she works in

Business Consulting and is inclined on curating novel people and culture-centric ideas.

Her unique perspective on slow-living shines through in her current writing. Through "Echoes of Existence," she strives to emphasize on the mundane and simplistic things in life that we usually overlook. She believes that we can find joy in the common, and her poetry attempts to unmask those areas of our life that hold the key to a happy well-being.

You can connect with Ritika through Instagram (@readablyours) as well as through her website (www.readablyours.com) to learn more about her work and stay updated on upcoming projects.